Embracing Life's Lessons

Journey to inner peace and tranquility

Stephanie E. Wilson

The Champagne Connection

Also by Stephanie E. Wilson

❤ ❤ ❤ ❤ ❤

Is Anybody Listening?

Life is too short to drink
Cheap Champagne seminar series

Embracing Life's Lessons

Copyright © 2004 by Stephanie E. Wilson
All rights Reserved.
No part of this book may be reproduced in any form or by any means, without permission in writing from the publisher.

Photographs by Bryant Johnson,
Steelelife Gallery, Chicago, IL

Cover design by Margaretta Henry

ISBN: 0-9749387-0-X

The Champagne Connection, Chicago, Illinois

Printed in the United States

From the Author's Heart . . .

DEDICATION

This book is dedicated to Imani Kali Henry, who reminded me to capture the joy in every moment and Lester Coleman, who has captured my heart.

From the Author's Heart . . .

ACKNOWLEDGEMENTS

I acknowledge all the women whose story I tell when I tell my own;

I acknowledge the tears of all women, for we never cry a single tear;

I acknowledge the arduous road traveled by all women in the search for equality;

I acknowledge the women who have gone before me and those who will come after me.

From the Author's Heart . . .

AUTHOR'S NOTES

It's been four years since my first book, *Is Anybody Listening?*, was published and I can truly say that life has been extremely interesting and filled with a multitude of change.

I've learned over and over that we achieve exactly what we believe we can achieve, no more, no less and that all of our challenges and tribulations are tailored made for us, by us. I have also learned that trusting the God-Mind that dwells within us does not always mean we that we will be able to judge righteously for there will be times when we allow ourselves to be betrayed by appearances.

Professionally, since my first book, I have completed the Executive MBA program at the University of Chicago and received a Master of Business Administration degree. I continue to serve as a motivational speaker and Life Coach with The Champagne Connection and best of all I have remarried.

In my travels as a motivational speaker, I constantly met people who allowed their past experiences to determine their future success. Because of this, I decided to write a book, biographical in content, that would prove that no one has a monopoly on the "bad weather" in our lives. We all have been subjected to the

cosmic 2 X 4, and in my life sometimes I needed a 6 X 8 for me to truly begin to trust the plan and purpose for my life. *Embracing Life's Lessons* is the result. By sharing a few of the events of my life, I hope to demonstrate that we can overcome all of the effects of life's experiences.

My prayer is that everyone who reads these lessons will realize their Divine inheritance and simply begin to use all of the great gifts from heaven.

Remember, life is too short to drink cheap champagne.

From the Author's Heart . . .

STRANGE HAPPENINGS

Had I known . . .
The trials of teenage motherhood would reveal worlds I never knew existed. I would not have complained, for it was meant for good.

Had I known . . .
The residue from sexual molestation and rape would serve as fuel propelling me to heights thought statistically impossible, I would not have complained, for it was meant for good.

Had I know . . .
The many crucifixions I endured due to my race and gender would result in resurrections that mimicked the rise of the Phoenix, I would not have complained, for it was mean for good.

Had I known . . .
Every transgression was woven with the golden threads of triumph, I would not have complained, for I would have realized I was surrounded by blessings.

—Stephanie E. Wilson

From the Author's Heart . . .

COMMENTS

Embracing Life's Lessons is a practical book by Stephanie E. Wilson, showing how life's lessons can be of help to you, the reader. It is an essential book for you to have as it helps the reader to appreciate life's lessons. As you embrace these lessons positively, you will find gems in this book, exciting chapters, e.g. Magical Intervention, Forgiveness, Walk in Beauty, Cracks in My Armor, Back to Basics and many more. You must invest in this book as you embrace your life's lessons in living.

—Rev. Whilmetta D. Harrell, Staff Minister, Christ Universal Temple, Chicago, IL

What a marvelous work. Words cannot express the inner peace I achieved through the affirmations in this book during my campaign for Judicial office.

—The Honorable Judge David Atkins
Chicago, IL

Contents

As the Sun Rises — 13
Starting each day with praise and thanksgiving connects your heart to the goodness of life.

Holding On — 19
Asking the "right" questions will reveal valuable information regarding your soul's growth.

Thou Shalt not Steal — 25
Your words are the secret to your success; do not allow them to steal your prosperity.

Forgiveness — 31
Forgiveness will eliminate hardened conditions and create a life filled with magnificent abundance; give yourself the gift of forgiveness.

Hard Hat Life — 37
When you do not know what to do, be still and watch the miracles happen.

Magical Intervention — 43
The magic begins in your mind, shaped by your words and molded by your actions.

Memories — 49
Only hold onto memories that are filled with love.

One Law — 55
Whatever captures your focus will shape the landscape of your life.

Dancing With Rage — 61
Conquering unresolved issues are the steps required to manifest your dreams.

Walk in Beauty — 67
Take time to refocus in order to see the beauty that surrounds you.

Who Are We? — 73
We are the dreamings of the Universe.

Climb Every Mountain — 79
To dance with Spirit requires you to scale the mountains and valleys in your life.

Life's Unwelcomed Visitor — 85
Allow your heart to embrace the divinity in all people.

Back to Basics — 91
Speak your success into existence with your words and thoughts.

Cracks in My Armor — 97
Embrace your humanness; perfection is not the goal.

We Are All Beggars of Some Sort — 103
Beseeching Spirit for more is not the answer: Living your dreams requires action not begging.

The Problem — 109
Every minute you choose between your spiritual beliefs and your human beliefs. So choose wisely.

Without concern for results, perform the necessary action; surrendering all attachments, accomplish life's highest good.

—The Bhagavad Gita

As the Sun Rises

Every Sunday morning at 5:30 AM, I join a group of 15 people for a yoga class at the Lakefront. Each class leaves me rejuvenated and filled with a serenity impossible to describe. There is something anagogic about watching the sunrise; I, too, am filled with the same power. The events of our lives mimic the sun; we encounter both sunrises and sunsets with all our experiences.

The activity of getting ready to go to the Lake before daybreak is always the same. At 4:30 AM, thoughts of my sanity swirl through my mind. At 4:45 AM, as I wiggle into a pair of leggings and a T-shirt, I decide that since I am awake, I might as well go to yoga. After all, it is beneficial for me. By 5:10 AM, I am well on my way, wondering how I could have considered missing the sun's awakening. And by 6:00 AM, any reluctance to attend today's class has dissipated like dew caught in the face of a fresh new morning.

As we salute the sun, I am moved to give thanks for all that is right in my world. The yoga sun salutation includes 12 movements, one for each month, and as I move into each posture I thank Spirit for my dreams and desires, health and exuberance, family and friends, joys and sorrows.

Because I have met so many people living without dreams, I am grateful that not only are my dreams extraordinary, but from time to time, they are absolutely overwhelming. I am thankful I could never give up on my dreams, for to give up on my dreams is to give up on myself. I understand that to be able to be overwhelmed, you must possess a spirit full of life, adventure and determination. As the sun rises, I know I possess these qualities. In fact, we all do.

I give thanks for my health. During the week, so many people cross my path that are in need of a physical healing. I have close friends who live everyday of their lives with the trials of stomach cancer, pancreatic cancer and brain tumors. It has not been that long ago I battled a deadly prognosis. The Universe returned to me

Embracing Life's Lessons

the gift of health, and I am ecstatic. So I give a double thanks to the sun.

Because we grow through people and projects, I give thanks for my family and friends. I give thanks because I have finally discovered the secret to happiness, love and peace. My need for peace far outweighs my need to be right, therefore, I am thankful for those in my life who think I am wonderful, and also for those who are always critical. We are all children of the "sun" with the need to give love and the desire to be loved. I accept all persons as the perfection they were created from and move onto the next experience.

Kahlil Gibran says the thing that fills you with sorrow is the other side of the thing that fills with you joy. With this in mind, I gave thanks for my joys and celebrated my sorrows.

After the class ends, my spirit is ablaze with excitement, and I am engulfed by reasons to celebrate my life. It is no surprise the problems I carried with me to the Lake are now distant and inconsequential.

When you find yourself stumped by negative energy and experiences, staying focused on all that is right in your world is the key to renewal.

Meditation/Affirmative Prayer

As I rise to greet each day, I allow all of the energy contained in the sun and its rays to penetrate and rejuvenate each cell within my body.

I choose this day to think only thoughts designed to align my body functions with the complete and perfect Love of the Divine Mind.

I accept the perfection of the sun and endeavor to embody it in all I think, do and say.

With an attitude of gratitude, I release my words to the Universe and I let it be so.

from my heart . . .

Come unto me, all ye that labor and are heavy laden, and I will give you rest.
For my yoke is easy and my burden is light.
—Matthew 11:28,30

Holding On

The other day one of my friends was talking about how much she needed her antidepressants and after reading my first book she was convinced I had some special protection from depression. I had to laugh. I shared with her a dark secret: any day I did not contemplate suicide was a good day. When I told her this, she replied, "But you are always so positive and upbeat." I said thank you. I explained that when I am not feeling positive, pleasant and upbeat, I stay home. It is during these times that I have to protect me from myself. Naturally, she asked what I did to survive these periods without the help of medication. Recognizing the urgency of her question, I knew she needed a direct, clear response. The answer had to be easy to understand and implement, not one filled with quasi-metaphysical religious jumbo.

Here is my technique. Every day I find some time, even if it is just 2 or 3 minutes, to acknowledge the blessings I have received. I take time to give thanks for warm shelter, a peaceful home environment, and friends—although they are not perfect—who are kind to me and thoughtful of me. I thank Spirit for my health, for the opportunity to watch the sunrise, and for allowing me to smell the many fragrances of the earth. Daily mini-praise services to Spirit are diligent guards against storms pushing to form in my life. They protect me from illness, depression and dis-ease in any form.

When I am having a "suicidal" or depressed moment, I concentrate heavily upon the many gifts and joys that are a part of my life. It is during these times I recall the things that enliven my soul and make my heart sing. I give thanks for my health, the health of my family and friends, being able to afford food, shelter and an occasional night out. I recall all the challenges I have faced and conquered: teenage parenthood, unemployment, homelessness and sexual abuse. I remember I am able to breath unencumbered, walk without assistance, and all my bodily functions are in perfect working order. Nor do I have the added burden of foreign entities entering my body threatening to end my life. After this, I reclaim my power by acknowledging I am the one who decides whether or not I will be happy, sad or depressed. I also remind myself that emotions are my counselors. Their sole purpose is to highlight areas in my life needing improvement. In other words, they come to guide and to bless, not to destroy. Because these intense feelings are here to aid me, I ask: What am I supposed to learn, instead of why me; or what is wrong with me; or why I can't get this right? By asking to have the lesson revealed, my mind is prepared for growth. In order to evolve and expand our consciousness, upward progression is mandatory. For even in nature, the things that do not evolve or adapt, wither and die.

So the next time you are having a "moment," get a pencil, lots of paper and begin asking the right questions. The Universe is patiently waiting to guide you.

Meditation/Affirmative Prayer

I thank you, Spirit, for all that you have given me. I thank you for a loving family, a peaceful home and for the daily discovery of new talents and skills. I thank you most of all for the power to choose.

Today, I choose to see Your blessings in the midst of all I encounter. I choose to see only the love and joy in my life.

As I surrender my errant thoughts, I know I will find rest in You.

from my heart . . .

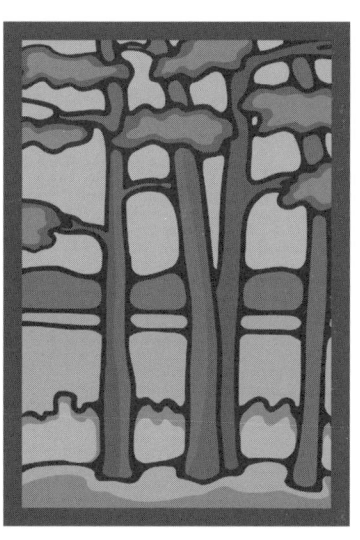

You must speak straight so that your words may go as sunlight to our hearts.

—Cochise, Cherokee Warrior

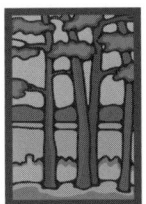

Thou Shalt Not Steal

Last week, as one of my yoga classes ended, we had an invigorating conversation about the Ten Commandments, focusing on "thou shalt not steal." Webster's defines the word "steal" as to take the property of another without right or permission. The word "another" is defined as one of an undetermined number or group. Using the Webster's definition allows us to take this commandment much further than stealing the property of others.

Most people in a civilized society are morally opposed to taking the property of others without expressed permission. We have enacted ordinances and laws in order to protect the members of our society. But what have we done to prevent us from stealing from the most important person in our lives, ourselves?

In order to answer this question, first list the ways in which we steal or deprive ourselves.

We steal our health by refusing to eat healthy well-balanced meals, not drinking enough water, overindulging in alcohol or other stimulants, ignoring our body's requirement for sufficient rest and not exercising our bodies daily. We constantly allow our words to damage our health by having "organ recitals" with our friends and neighbors, testifying to our failing health and aching muscles. With zeal, we declare the poor condition of our health by repeating over and over "I do not feel well" or "I feel like I am catching something."

We steal our peace of mind by not meditating or relaxing at frequent intervals, believing that it is our responsibility to solve the problems of our loved ones and by participating and facilitating gossip.

We steal our prosperity by speaking untrue statements, such as, I am broke; I do not have any money; I cannot afford it; some people have all the luck; other folk have all the fun. Our spoken word is one of the most powerful creative tools we have. Therefore, every time we say things regarding our wealth or lack of, we are sending orders into a Universe that has no choice but to create the very thing declared. The Law of

Attraction and the Law of Cause and Effect guarantee that what we send out will return to us. Genesis states that our word will not return to us void.

Our actions also determine our experiences. When we neglect to perform at our very best, we send a message to the Universe that we expect less than the best.

In what ways are you stealing from yourself? What messages are you sending forth?

This week spend some time thinking about the instances you steal from yourself. List them and start to eliminate them one at a time.

When I recommitted to watching my words and guarding my thoughts, I was surprised at the number of times I could see myself in the examples. With a renewed sense of purpose, I practice prosperity in my own life.

Meditation/Affirmative Prayer

In the magic of this moment, I acknowledge and release the power I have given to the various creations of fear. As I refuse to indulge in any self-inflicted acts of violence, such as over-eating, negative and traitorous self-talk or gossip, the nightmare of all binding and restrictive thought is dissolved and reincarnated as a direct connection to the Goodness of Spirit.

From this day forward, my actions support my positive core beliefs.

From this day forward, my words fortify the things I wish to experience, and my world is flooded with all the good I can imagine.

from my heart . . .

Forgiveness is the first requirement which permits man to be in harmony with the Law of his being.

—Working with the Law, Raymond Holliwell

Forgiveness

Well, it had happened to me again.

It had been a long time since I had met someone who was able to push my buttons to the point that I wanted to throw them out of a window. I actually found myself dreaming of ways to inflict damage, both physical and mental. I guess you could say I was having a moment, a touch of humanness. In the midst of this conflict, I found it difficult to live my own principles. Even worse, I had to admit I secretly enjoyed these unspeakable flights of fancy. I felt as though I deserved the right to wallow in these transgressions.

But life is good.

One night, during my meditation, I realized I did not really want to cause any harm. I simply wanted to be released, to be rid of him. I instantly understood I was going to have to find a way to forgive him and myself for this human infraction. I knew I had to forgive the person and the circumstances immediately. But none of the forgiveness techniques I used in the past were working. Bewildered and a bit disheartened, I kept trying and without flash or fanfare the answer was revealed.

Following the guidance I received, I affirmed, "through the forgiving power of Jesus Christ, I forgive and release (the person's name) and they forgive and release me. All lessons are learned, all blessing have been received and it is over." I repeated this affirmation three times at the beginning of each hour. By the fifth hour I could actually feel my intense anger begin to diminish. Every time I found myself thinking about this situation, I refocused my attention and visualized the love of the Universe wrapped around both of us, and repeated the affirmation. The next week, as I interacted with my nemesis, I continued to be plagued with so much anguish I wanted to scream. Instead, I silently repeated this affirmation and reminded myself that we both are perfect creations of the Divine. By the end of the second week, I noticed I could engage in a conversation with this person without wanting to cause harm. Excitement flowed through me. I could feel my soul shouting "hallelujah, thank you Spirit."

This experience was another reminder of Spirit's completeness and power. By surrendering my thoughts to the One Presence and Power, by thinking as Spirit would think, I was able to transcend this situation.

Every day is filled with castle-building experiences and perfect opportunities to prove the perfect goodness of Spirit. We decide, by our thoughts and actions, if our experiences will reflect peace or turmoil. <u>Forgiveness is a gift we give to ourselves. It has nothing to do with the other person.</u>

Meditation/Affirmative Prayer

I am surrounded by everything I need to manifest my dreams and desires. Everyone I meet and every situation I encounter on my journey to wholeness is my teacher. As I embrace my healing, thoughts of anger or any others like it, dissipate as I acknowledge that there is only One Presence and Power in my life and affairs.

All experiences are created by me for the sole purpose of highlighting any growth areas within my consciousness. I embrace this information simply as a signal to learn new skills, therefore, there is nothing to forgive for, in truth, everything works for good.

from my heart . . .

Whither shall I go from thy Spirit? Or whither shall I flee from thy presence?
If I ascend up to heaven, thou art there: if I make my bed in hell, behold, thou art there.

—Psalms 139: 7,8

Hard Hat Life

I stood at the apex of an experience for which I was ill-prepared to address. As I wrote, my soul was tossed about like a ship trapped in the heart of a hurricane. Shipwrecked is the appropriate word to describe how I felt. I was unable to put my words on paper, they had been captured by legions of silence. Frightened, I turned to my significant other for support, hoping to find the anchor to calm my soul, hoping to save my sanity, only to have him betray me with refusal, but not before suggesting that correcting my less than positive thoughts is the raft I should cling to and I should just comply with "God's" will. The inference that thinking positively could somehow circumvent my grieving and the suggestion that complying with God's will is as easy as breathing, seemed impossible. If this were true, our human experience would not be a smorgasbord filled with an assortment of lack, limitation, sorrow, joy, health, disease, prosperity and poverty. I realized I was forced to travel alone, forced to embrace an experience that had depleted my energy and imprisoned my soul.

Life, however, requires you to "do what you have to do," even if you have to do it alone. Both our individual and collective race consciousness serves as the catalyst which molds the conditions we battle in our human experience, i.e., abject poverty, racism, aging, etc. Knowing this did not ease the turmoil, but like Paul, even though I was encamped on all sides, I was not defeated.

In order to triumphantly survive the experience, I concentrated on keeping my heart open by allowing myself to experience all of the feelings that clung to this "moment" like a two-year-old does to its mother. I did not expect to be immune from the valley or basement experiences brewing as a result of our race consciousness. I only needed to appreciate the magic in everyday ordinary life. This alone would be enough to be spiritually aligned with the Divine, enough to prove the existence of Spirit in my life, and I believe our primary reason for existing is to prove the existence of Spirit in our lives.

Believing life itself is the miracle, I stopped flooding the ethers with prayers, requests for divine intervention and even affirmations. Realizing that it was not up to me to deem a situation to be a success or a failure, good or bad, prosperous or limited, I began to look at all conditions under the sun as good. Before now, I would have never thought illness, poverty, imprisonment, marginal performance or the like a blessing, but if life itself is the miracle, then all the things we find in life are an expression of this miracle. Outer conditions reflect the rumble and tumble of life and we must remember to condemn the "sin and not the sinner." By judging conditions that appear in our physical experience, we have positioned ourselves to be both conciliator and executioner and this is not our assignment.

As truth students, we have a tendency to affirm "good" experiences and deny the "bad" ones. But true Metaphysicians understand that concluding one experience is better than another gives power to outer conditions. If we are to truly find the good in all things, we must be reminded to "judge not by experiences" but to see Spirit in the midst of all things.

Meditation/Affirmative Prayer

As I find myself in the middle of a storm, not knowing which way to turn, I focus on Jesus, the Christ, and speak the words "PEACE BE STILL." Grateful for the calm seas that are the result of my command, I now redirect my attention to the true miracles.

Remembering that what I do with my life is my gift to God, my mind is inundated with ways to prove the power and existence of the Indwelling Christ in my life. Keeping my heart open and my vision clear, I celebrate the good in all situations, for Spirit is evenly and equally everywhere present.

I refuse to judge situations. Instead, I approach challenges with faith that can move mountains. I lift the veil clouding my view and I am awakened to the abundance that surrounds and enfolds me.

from my heart . . .

Your mind is your world. Your thoughts are the tools with which you carve your life's story on the substance of the universe. When you rule your mind, you rule your world. When you choose your thoughts, you choose results.

—Imelda Shanklin

Magical Invention

As I sat in this holy place of worship surrounded by the latest couture, perfectly coifed hairstyles and fresh manicures, my mind would not easily be quieted. I expected magic to ooze through the ethers, attach itself to my dis-ease and inject an enchanted elixir that would result in an instant cure. I do not know how long I sat and listened and waited before I realized that no matter how intense my desire, there would be no magical intervention. Was this a sign that the light at the end of the tunnel had been temporarily disconnected? As I communed with my internal voices, I overheard a conversation that abruptly interrupted my thoughts. Because I was mentally driving a train headed for destruction, I decided to focus on what was happening around me.

A man sitting a few rows in front of me seemed overwhelmed by despair. His mother had made her transition just a few days before, leaving him clothed in grief. For years, I had seen his mother once a week, never anticipating or expecting her transition. Because of this natural event, her son had been unwillingly tossed into an experience he was at best ill-prepared to handle. As I studied him, he tossed fretfully back and forth in his seat. He, too, was hoping for some supernatural occurrence to soothe his pain and calm his thoughts.

The next soul had a different tale. At 85 years old, he experienced a fall. Fortunately, his fall was minor, in that he sustained a small fracture in one of the bones in his left foot. As I eavesdropped, he was indeed grateful for he knew at his age falls usually result in a broken hip which may be a gateway to death for the elderly. He, however, had another concern, a much more pressing issue. It was the recent discovery that his wife, his long time companion, friend, lover and mother of his children, had a terminal illness. Her prognosis was not good and for the first time in his life, this unexpected chain of events had redirected the course of his life. He, too, waited for some magical intervention.

In the midst of my reverie, I spotted a man who was so handsome he looked like something good to eat. I studied his hard body, chiseled face and bedroom eyes. But he, too, was struggling

Embracing Life's Lessons

with his thoughts. Having never married or fathered children, his entire world was constructed around his parents. He loved them dearly; it was their love, constant support and deep belief in his ability that served as the catalyst for his success, and he had achieved more than he ever thought possible. His parents celebrated his achievements and lovingly corrected his errors. As Tony Morrison said about the people living in the town of Medallion (*Sula*), birth may be accidental, but not death. It was natural. He had lost both parents within weeks of each other and for the first time in his life he was alone. He, too, longed for some psychic event.

As I nestled in the arms of the thoughts of the people around me, I looked closer at my concerns. My thoughts did not contain any residue of death, betrayal, illness or sorrow. I was preoccupied with events that appeared mediocre and unimportant when stacked against some of the teeth-rattling experiences in my past. I have worked diligently in demonstrating the power of truth in my life in the face of good and evil and have overcome many events, situations and unexpected challenges. I am grateful.

My overcoming was possible not by magical intervention, but by a concerted effort to control my thoughts, starve the mental meanderings that predicted despair, master my spiritual powers and build my faith. As I started to savor the good present in my life, I felt the "funk" disintegrate. The magical intervention I longed for was present all the time.

Meditation/Affirmative Prayer

I greet this day enthusiastically and zealously knowing that I am in complete control of all that happens. I celebrate, knowing that if I crave a different outcome, I simply change my thoughts.

Because there is no power in the past or the future, I center all my attention, thoughts and actions on the events of today. As I approach all occurrences, I remove the veil of despair and I remind myself that I am looking into the face of God.

from my heart . . .

Man must not allow the clock and the calendar to blind him to the fact that each moment of your life is a miracle and a mystery.

—H.G. Wells

Memories

In the movie *After Life*, upon death, everybody was asked to recall their best memory. I found this question so intriguing that I posed it to a group of friends at my birthday dinner party. Like me, they were unable to isolate just one memory. As the night moved on, we found ourselves eagerly sharing our lives, using our joyful experiences and painful tales as threads on the bridges of the lives we have created.

After the dinner party, still intrigued by this question, rest alluded me until I began to record some of the memories that were like melodies created by Brahm. Because I have dreamed countless dreams, I wondered what would be revealed to me, about me, by these invisible companions. I was determined to sift through the dreams and flirt with the memories that have shaped this event I call my life.

As a teenage mother, memories of these years are bittersweet at best, however I continue to discover gems from this experience. In spite of the negative vibrations that surrounded me at that time, I have endless heart-warming memories of my son. He was then and continues to be the wind beneath my wings.

As I continued this journey through my past, I remembered my seventh grade math teacher who insisted I give my all. I remember walking barefoot through grassy meadows, climbing trees to pick apples and hiding from imagined dangers as we searched the wooded areas for blackberries. I remember playing dress up in my cousin's Sunday shoes, using the good pans to make mud pies, jumping Double Dutch and dancing "the pony" on top of the living room furniture. I remember daytime soaps, sneaking to watch Johnny Carson and singing with little Stevie Wonder, "If I had a childhood sweetheart." I also remember being robbed of my innocence with the assassination of Malcolm X, John F. Kennedy and Martin Luther King, Jr.

I remember not being certain I could make it after my divorce. But I remember most, those who showed up in my life to make certain I did. I remember the friends who would listen as long as I needed them, too, and the few who would spend hours playing in make-up just to help me pass the time.

I remember feeling like a complete failure when I lost my job, my home and my car. But I remember most, the people who dried my tears as I wept. I remember breathtaking sunsets, picture perfect sunrises and Infinite Kindness opening my soul to the "truth" about who I am.

When I moved thousands of miles away from home, I remember being unbearably cold, dreadfully homesick and incredibly confused. But I also remember the precious few who warmed my heart, brightened my smile, fueled my laughter, appreciated the true essence of who I am and loved me in spite of humanness.

The more I remember, the more I realize that no matter what our memories are made up of, they are all wrapped with gems of happiness, filled with the presence of angels, and saturated with more love than we will ever know.

Remember life is too short to drink cheap champagne.

Meditation/Affirmative Prayer

It is often said the present moment is our only point of power. That means each day and every moment is filled with beauty and pregnant with unlimited possibilities.

Today is not only the first day of the rest of my life, it is a gift from the Universe stuffed full of memorable experiences and endless opportunities to choose my destiny.

As I go through my daily activities, I promise myself I will take a few seconds every hour to allow my many blessings to permeate my spirit. As I choose my direction, today I choose love, I choose joy, I choose peace and I watch the rest fade away.

from my heart . . .

To the question of your life, you are the only answer. To the problems of your life, you are the only solution

—Jo Coudert

One Law

As I sat in my car waiting for the light to change, I was gripped so deeply in thought, I nearly missed the change of signal. Solicitously reviewing the troubling scenarios currently playing in my life, I felt the heaviness of a seemingly impossible situation intruding into my conscious thoughts, causing me to wonder if this would ever pass, causing me to doubt if I had the wherewithal to persevere. Suddenly, without warning, I heard James Cleveland singing, "Where Is Your Faith?" Because my radio was not on, I knew this was a cosmic newsbreak. The fullness of this man's voice caused me to abandon my negative thoughts and focus solely on his words. As I thought about this song, a lesson from the Course of Miracles dashed across my mind. This particular lesson is one that teaches us that we are under one law—Spirit's law.

Because we are so busy creating from our human consciousness, we unknowingly make laws out of things in the outer, thereby, relinquishing our power. I was buying heavily into the race consciousness thought system and seemed to be eager to trade my spiritual awareness as collateral. There I sat, a truth student for nearly ten years, believing that I would not prosper unless certain human conditions existed. Not only did I believe this, I was carefully organizing and sorting out all the details. I believed, because society said, I could not own the home or business of my dreams. After all, everyone knows those things are just too expensive. The human consciousness believes you are lonely if you do not have people and lovers in your life; if you do not eat right and exercise you will be sick. I, like everyone else, had made laws out of jobs, people, lovers, friends, material possessions, nutrition, exercise and money.

As I continued to ponder this truth, I remembered the promise and the only requirement is to seek first the kingdom of God and all things will be added to you. The more I meditated on this, the more I understood that Spirit's law is the only law. Having a life filled with great health, abundant prosperity, endless love and bountiful miracles has nothing to do with outer human consciousness. Spirit has given us these things because Spirit truly loves us, even when we miss the mark. Because we are created by Love, the state of any human condition means absolutely nothing.

As my "Spirit moment" continued, I remembered a short verse in the Old Testament . . . Is anything too hard for God? No. The hard part is actually the easiest.

Everything appearing in our lives has a mental companion. My only effort, then, is to work with my consciousness. As I began again to remove the veil from the opulence Spirit has already given me and turn a deaf ear to all the things outside myself, in the blink of an eye, I will create, once more, things that are in keeping with my true identity. Nothing is impossible to those who focus on the promises of Creative Mind.

Meditation/Affirmative Prayer

Just for today, I will keep my mind filled with possibilities, not obstacles. I will trust that Power greater than myself to guide and direct my steps. I will keep my conversations filled with the good I deserve and watch this goodness engulf me. I will seek out the things that make my soul smile and take time to appreciate the beauty that surrounds me.

Just for today, I seek to create a life through my connection and partnership with Spirit. I will believe, just for today, that the Universal power is working to shape my world in ways that I cannot begin to imagine.

Just for today, nothing will be impossible.

Just for today, I will not be separated from God.

from my heart . . .

Each of us makes his own weather, determines the color of the skies in the emotional universe which he inhabits.

—Fulton J. Sheen

Dancing With Rage

Last week I was jarred from a peaceful nap by a presence so haunting that I was unable to go back to sleep. I found myself as a teenager filled with intolerable pain that was born of sexual abuse. I felt surrounded by people telling me I was not worthy. The longer I lay in bed the more intense this feeling became. Remnants of other experiences wasted no time crowding my thoughts in support of my agony. The knowledge that this unwelcome presence was created by my own intimate thoughts did not make it any easier to bear. These emotions were molded from events I never allowed myself to talk about or share with others. I now know that our "little secrets" have the power to ruin our lives if we do not confront them.

I've spent years trying to maintain a balance in this event called life. Working to experience the joys as well as the sorrows of life had kept me centered—until that moment.

As tears rolled down my face, the weight of these horrid memories with their painful emotions riding shotgun, were agonizing. But a force within me would not let me retreat. This loving Spirit reminded me that It is not merely a part of my life, but is my life.

I have always believed if we focus on Spirit when we are in the midst of turmoil, we will be able to overcome anything. So not knowing what else to do, I waited for this Infinitely Kind Being to comfort me.

It was this experience that reminded me that just as Jesus was tested, we will also be tested. Our assignment is to remember the Omniscient Presence in all things. As we step into our divinity and continue our journey hand in hand with our Indwelling Christ, any unresolved issues in our consciousness will come forward. Because opposites cannot occupy the same space, we will always be required to grow, required to change and required to release any emotions unlike "love," no matter the experience.

As I waited to be comforted, I knew Spirit would never fail me or forsake me. I permitted myself to feel these bitter and angry emotions and explore them thoroughly. I envisioned them enfolded with love and I felt them dissipate. Like a good parent, Infinite Kindness stayed with me until my spirit was free. Now, when I try to recall these emotions, I find only love—love for myself and love for Spirit.

Meditation/Affirmative Prayer

In this moment in time we are perfect, unencumbered by the trials of yesterday and the tribulations of tomorrow. Unaffected by the fantasies of lack, limitation and error thoughts that plague our past and derail our future, we embrace this fleeting second of wholeness.

Divinely inspired, we understand this precious second is our only point of power. In this precious second, we begin to sow the seeds that will serve as the foundation of our tomorrows.

Because each life is painted with moments just like this one, let us use our moments and our power to celebrate our perfection forever stalling any challenges we might otherwise create.

In this moment, we are not limited by time, space or circumstances, for in this moment we are divinely guided.

from my heart . . .

Beauty is eternity gazing at itself in a mirror.
But you are eternity and you are the mirror.

—The Prophet, Kahlil Gibran

Walk in Beauty

Two mornings in a row I witnessed a sight so beautiful, I was convinced if Renoir was still alive he would have painted this scene to ensure the image would be etched in the hearts and souls of all throughout the ages. I have always believed there was magic in mornings, today I am convinced.

Because the last two days have been extremely cold, I rushed out of the house completely wrapped in outer garments, wondering how one could experience any joy in these frigid conditions. It took all the energy I could gather just to survive the walk to the car. As I traveled to my destination, I considered going back home and staying in bed until the break of spring. No matter how compelling this idea seemed, I had to admit it was not practical. Besides, my human needs could not be satisfied without venturing outside.

While waiting for the traffic light to turn green, anxious to get out of all this cold, snow and ice, I saw it. On my right, nestled along the lake was a snow-covered building that seemed to reach up to kiss the sky. As the clouds extended its cover to this lone building, it appeared to be perfectly backlit with the sun's rays. Chunks of ice and snow-blanketed stray branches, seemingly hand-placed, filled the surface of the lake. The water appeared still, full of life, but still nonetheless. Placed perfectly throughout the ice and around the building were geese, hundreds of them, huddled in small groups to generate warmth. It was perfect. I reflected on this stunning sight all day, never expecting to see it again. So when I saw it the next morning my joy could not be contained. Blind to the outer appearance of brutal cold stood a sight of extreme beauty that personified peace. This is exactly what we must do in our lives.

Spirit created us so It could enjoy more of Itself through us. Because we are the only hands, feet and hearts Spirit has, it is up to us to stand firm, radiating beauty, while transcending any negatives surrounding us. To speak healing words filled with life, no matter where you find

Embracing Life's Lessons

yourself, is the key to dissolving negative appearances. Treat all negative appearances as you would if they were gifts given to you wrapped in beautiful paper. Work with negative appearances as you would unwrap a gift, removing the stickiness, one piece at a time. Expect a fantastic surprise, an answer to your prayers to be hidden within this "strange wrapping paper." Everything that appears on your journey has come to bless you, teach you who you really are, and help you identify the skills you need so you may live your dreams. Expecting a gift will keep you at the mountaintop of consciousness and open you to inner guidance and raise your consciousness so you can manifest the blessings that are on the horizon awaiting your awakening.

Today, I walk in beauty.

Meditation/Affirmative Prayer

Knowing that which I see is what I will receive, I expand my vision beyond the physical until I connect with the spiritual.

As I come closer to Spirit, I am drawn into Its field of love and all that is unlike Spirit is dissolved and transformed into pure Opulence.

Knowing that the Creative Force of this grand Universe is limitless, inexhaustible and understanding, I release my concerns, knowing it is already done.

from my heart . . .

. . . We are powerful beyond measure . . .
—Nelson Mandela

Who We Are

Sweet Honey in the Rock sings, for each child that's born, a morning star rises and sings to the Universe who we are: we are our grandmothers' prayers, we are our grandfathers' dreamings, we are the breath of the Universe, we are the spirit of God. We are mothers of courage . . . sons of great visions . . . seekers of truth.

This has been a week of intense introspection and divine discontent. As I look ahead in anticipation of the upcoming years by revisiting various episodes of my life, the actions needed to live my dreams and empower my loved ones remain as elusive as the cure for AIDS. It seems I am no better walking my talk than I was two years ago. My life is still filled with challenges, and I find I am constantly in need of a resurrection. There has been one thing I can count on. Nothing will remain the same. Every single thing will change and sometimes the appearance it takes will rattle the calmness of the soul. If my career is going great, then my children were buying property on fools' hill or vice versa. But because all thoughts, experiences and paths lead to Spirit, Sweet Honey in the Rock reminds me just who I am, a seeker of truth.

As I put my experiences into perspective in order to see my next step, I know everything happens as a direct result of our relationship with the Universe. Every time we learn a truth, the race consciousness will create an event that will challenge this new truth causing us to get up close and personal with our belief, searching our souls and minds for any weakness.

Because the Universe is magnanimous in Its giving, we must relinquish all little ideas we have in our subconscious regarding our existence. The desires of our heart is the Universe seeking a greater expression of Itself through us. Being guided by these Divine promptings requires faith. Letting go of our limited concept of our achievements requires courage. But until we eagerly and willingly embrace Life's gifts we will never fully comprehend the truth about who we are.

Embracing Life's Lessons

Understanding that as a seeker of Truth I will always encounter challenges has made my day-to-day journey joyful. The very nature of a Truth seeker is to move beyond the appearances and the success of today. If I do not do this, I become restless and my soul becomes dehydrated. My need to push the limits and move to a higher level causes me to keep my focus well beyond the horizon, constantly amazing myself at how much I am able to achieve. So I go forth today, looking beyond appearances, filled with a faith that can move mountains, dwelling in the harmony of Spirit, as I watch my experiences shift into pure opulence and unlimited abundance.

Meditation/Affirmative Prayer

As I celebrate the Omnipotent Presence, I embrace the evolution of Life.

As I open my mind and allow my soul to reach toward the Divine, I eagerly accept my higher calling knowing that change is a prerequisite for growth.

As I reach toward my hearts desire, I now discard all limiting beliefs and ideas.

With a faith that can move mountains, I am filled with an inner knowing that all I can see is mine.

from my heart . . .

*The end of all our exploring
will be to arrive where we start
and know that place for the first time*

—t.s. elliot

Climb Every Mountain

As I listened to various confessions filled with tales of woe, the pain saturating the room and encircling my spirit was as thick as molasses in the middle of a Midwest winter. The more vivid the remembrances of betrayal, the heavier my heart sank. As members of this group of thirty-something singles recalled in vivid detail various valley experiences, I was drawn to dance with their pain, hide in its shadows, and bathe in its fragrance. Climbing the many mountains encountered on these multiple journeys had been, in the least, a hard climb. Mixed in the liquid pain was the sweet, sticky, but most often misunderstood, aroma of forgiveness.

For a brief moment in time, we betrayed life as we flirted with memories long gone, when we were in a different time, being someone we have since forgotten. As I inhaled the fumes of this lethal emotion, I was drawn into the cesspool of my own battles, crucifixions and tribulations. I was hypnotized and momentarily unable to withdraw from this drunken state. I was drowning in the very waters I had spent my life mastering. Because I am considered a motivator, others often believe that I am too enlightened to be filled with painful experiences and feelings, however, at this moment, like none other before, I fully comprehended the dangers of dwelling in the past.

If we are to have any future at all, living in the present moment is a must. This makes forgiveness a necessary ingredient for our survival and controlling our thoughts a prerequisite for complete happiness.

I have quoted Ernest Holmes often as saying our thoughts are tools with the power to bless or destroy. Any adversity we experience is directly related to how well we master this tool. This is not to imply the past is of no importance, for it is a significant portion of who we are. It must be embraced, loved, and reconciled, if we are ever going to fully express our true spiritual nature. It is in our reconciliation, our act of forgiveness that allows us to not only to forgive but to forget the pain associated with the memories. Because we cannot experience the whole spirit of the

Universe as a fragmented being, we cannot ignore the act of forgiveness. Spirit is absolute good and can only create good, therefore, Spirit cannot recognize anything unlike Itself. It does not recognize good or evil, greatness or littleness, wealth or poverty. We have been given the willpower to define these things for ourselves.

Once we have embraced the painful experiences, we are then able to emit an aura so powerful the trees will bow, the birds will sing, the daffodils will dance and all the gifts of the Universe will rise to greet us. Perhaps, this is why we are counseled in Philippians 4:8 to dwell on the things that are pure, just and of good report.

Meditation/Affirmative Prayer

As I gaze on the mountains that frame the landscape of this city, my thoughts lean toward the mountains in my life. In this quiet, private space, my soul is comforted by the visible peaks and valleys carved in the mountains. Just as the mountains are made more beautiful by the visible variety of experience, so is my soul.

Ernest Holmes states in *Living the Science of Mind*, "the mind that states a problem is the mind that knows the answer." Therefore, anytime a valley experience appears, the perfect answer appears in tandem.

With this in mind, I am reminded by the mountains within my view, that our human experience is filled with mountaintop and valley experiences. These interwoven experiences create as a by-product a life that is a constant testament to the Goodness of Spirit.

As I relax further into this moment, I realize that a life without challenges would leave me stagnant. And to dance with Spirit requires constant movement, growing, and changing.

With this awareness, I consciously connect to Spirit for a greater awareness of my spirituality.

from my heart . . .

*Life and death are one thread,
the same line viewed from different sides*

—Lao-tzu

Life's Unwelcome Visitor

Often, we spend moments on earth filling our days with activities designed simply to pass the time while keeping us from concentrating on the truly important issues. Soon, we begin to define our success in terms of material possessions and accomplishments. We become experts at structuring our activities so that we avoid life's kitchen table. Suddenly, something happens to jolt us; then we are forced to assess the criteria we use to determine achievements. We look at our life in terms of how much money we earn, the neighborhood we live in and the powerful people we know. We fail to use measuring tools that reveal the Truth—how much love, joy, peace and true prosperity we experience. It is not long before we realize we have neglected the most important and powerful aspect of our being, our soul.

For me it was death. Life was going great. Finally, I was making some impressive connections and mingling with people I longed to meet. Then suddenly, without warning, two of my close friends lost a parent. This forced me to reevaluate the value of my creations. I realized these mothers and fathers had lived their lives under my nose and I did not really know them. We never talked about their successes, failures, regrets, favorite colors, flowers or fragrances. I never knew the dreams now lost forever. I took them for granted and only now do I ask what was I to learn from them. Had I been too busy forcing "my will" that I overlooked someone precious, missed some valuable lesson? Had I become so self-absorbed in my own little dramas that I failed to recognized one of Spirit's rare unrepeatable gifts? The study of Truth requires me to intensely focus on forgiveness. Was I so busy forgiving my brother that I forgot to notice his divinity, to love him?

It is said that death is a tattletale. I am inclined to agree, for it speaks boldly about how we, and those close to us, live our lives. Through these deaths, I learned both people lived their lives fully, unhindered by illness. Everyday of their lives they freely gave of themselves to their children, spouses, friends and the friends of their children, taking nothing in return. They were living examples of the prayer uttered by St. Francis . . . I do not seek to be consoled as to console . . . to be loved as to love. We, on the other hand, devoured all they had to offer and never thought to refuel their spirits. We neglected to offer them the beauty of roses to gaze upon, to smell their intoxicating fragrances. We find ourselves as perfect personifications of Charles Dickens' Scrooge.

In our race consciousness, we are conditioned to take and take from others with no emphasis on giving of ourselves. By doing this, we avoid engaging in conversations of value with the people in our lives. Conversations around life's kitchen table are filled with gems of wisdom that fill our journey with joy as we travel through the maze of experiences we call life. They are filled with fables that should be passed from generation to generation and gender to gender. We must quiet our lives so we are able to listen to the stories, share the joy and help to heal the pain experienced by others. These are filled with blessings from the Creator and answers to some of the concerns plaguing our own consciousness.

Getting to know the various facets of every person in our life is our responsibility. By cementing into our hearts the very essence of their spirit, we are ensuring their immortality. As we allow our spirits to dance with each other, we become living examples of our "Oneness."

Meditation/Affirmative Prayer

As I celebrate the activity of each moment, I become more attuned to the lessons others are here to teach me.

I consciously look for the hidden gems in each encounter with another creation of the Divine.

Because God is the only Truth that exists, I joyously commune with the divinity in my brother.

from my heart . . .

Our individual world is a reflection of our thought life. We people it with hate and discord, or love and harmony, according to our thoughts.

—Henry Thomas Hamblin

Back to Basics

It is written, if you have faith as small as a mustard seed, you will move mountains and nothing will be impossible for you. It is also written, faith is the substance of things hoped for, the evidence of things not seen. What is not written is that faith is a five-letter word that is often spelled W-O-R-K.

The Course in Miracles states it is impossible not to believe what you see and equally impossible to see what you do not believe. Perceptions are built on the basis of experience, and experience leads to belief. Changing your beliefs so that you can change your experience requires consistent effort.

In order to manifest the many wonderful promises of the Universe, we must know what we want and accept it. Because we are intimately connected to the universal life force, whether we acknowledge it or not, we are creating experiences all the time. All creations start as thoughts, so we must first change our thoughts, expand our minds, enlarge our beliefs, and not focus on our behavior.

Too often we permit our thoughts to flirt with the most damnable circumstances. We allow our minds to contemplate our personal diaries of "what ifs." What if I lose my job, what if my husband is cheating on me, what if I have a dreadful disease. Then, we are flabbergasted when the very incident we mentally forecasted appears in our lives. It is difficult to constantly watch our thoughts, but necessary if we are to experience the true splendor Spirit has granted. Quickly, we must understand there is no such thing as an idle thought. All thought produces form at some level, therefore, negative thoughts are luxuries we cannot afford.

Since our thoughts trigger our words, the next phase is to guard our spoken word. The Book of Genesis gives us naming power and because we are made in the image and likeness of the Divine Creative Intelligence, our words will not return to us unfulfilled. This very image and likeness makes us all-powerful. It is this power that commands our thoughts and words to mold the universal substance into the very forms we speak of.

While we are comfortably pondering scenarios that are sure to lead us to hell, we force them into existence with our words by engaging in organ recitals with our friends—my bad knees, my swollen feet and, oh, my aching back. We then fuel the fire by declaring there is not enough money to go around, the economy is bad and nobody loves me. It should not come as a surprise when we are downsized, our health fails, or our husband elopes with our best friend.

Because words are packed with power, utmost caution must be exercised when we speak. Being cognizant of our words will limit the number of negative appearances we have to conquer. If this seems too difficult, remember everything you say must take root in the outer. If you honestly think back to a negative appearance, you will remember forecasting it.

By now you are wondering what could you possibly have to talk about? It is written, whatever things are true, noble, and of good report . . . meditate on these things. Because Spirit is equally present everywhere, it will not be long before true abundance is the norm and not the exception in your life.

Meditation/Affirmative Prayer

I rededicate myself to sowing thoughts that will harvest the dreams dancing in my soul.

Today, I will allow thoughts of prosperity, abundance and health simmer in my mind. I will think only things I want to experience.

Today, I rededicate myself to flirt only with unlimited possibilities.

from my heart . . .

Do not fear mistakes. There are none.

—Miles Davis

Cracks in My Armor

I was so excited when a publisher finally agreed to publish my first book that I could not eat or sleep for weeks. As a matter of fact, the publisher, an African-American woman, was more interested in my pseudo-metaphysical spiritual subject matter than I. However, none of my previous experiences prepared me for the feelings of inadequacy and anxiety that come along with having the cracks in your armor illumined and closely scrutinized. All I knew was I had finally found the faith to aggressively pursue the Divine nudgings that had been tugging at my heart for years. Even though I had worked on this project for what seemed like an eternity, I made a ton of mistakes and the error catchers were at the top of their game.

This mixture of anxiety and excitement made me somewhat unstable and slightly suicidal. My nerves were raw, my energy spent, and my soul depleted. I had a strong desire to run for cover. Minutes before my private book signing, I was told there were no books. The printer cut them incorrectly and the pages were completely screwed up. I hear time is a great healer and I am told that what does not kill you will make you strong; at this point, time was not moving fast enough and I was convinced I was near death. My girlfriend, my mentor, reminded me that if you do not have a test, you do not have a testimony. Somewhere in my book, *Is Anybody Listening?*, I write that we will not always live up to the expectations we have defined for our lives. I also remind the reader that life does not always go according to our plan because we are not the Master Planner. It was up to me to not only remember this lesson, but to live this lesson. So I forgave the detours and dealt with the problem. Talk about a character building experience.

At the book signing, I explained the errors and we had a party. We had a grand party. We celebrated each other. We toasted our success, laughed heartily at our failures and reminded each other that in our humanness, perfection should never be the goal. We acknowledge that just as we are, cracks and all, we all are a perfect expression of the Universe. Any reason to celebrate our oneness is a good reason.

When I woke up the next day, thinking about my book or lack thereof, I found myself filled with the presence of Spirit, Infinite Kindness and all was well. I knew I had not been forsaken, and if a leader in technology could survive the crash in front of the world, I could certainly handle this book fiasco.

We are in this human form to learn who we truly are. Expressing our Divine nature cannot be accomplished with one event, but is a process that will span our entire life. As I wrestled with this seeming failure, I realized in spite of all the problems, I was truly blessed. For the first time, I appeared vulnerable. My friends lovingly showered me with hugs, kisses and praises. They were grateful I allowed them to share this event with them. Finally, I had given them an opportunity to love me and tell me how important I was to them. I'll remember this day forever and if I ever get too "grand," just remind me of my first private book signing.

Meditation/Affirmative Prayer

As I begin this day, my heart is overflowing with a realization and deep understanding that the miracle I have been praying for has already manifested as the outward picturing of me. For I am filled with an unlimited capacity for love, simple imaginings that are the foundation of my abundance, and an instant connection with the Principle I call God—the balm that soothes and heals my soul.

Today, I will marvel at every expression of the Universe in all I see and hear, with all I meet and interact, with my blessings of yesterday and possibilities of tomorrow. Because I am Spirit's feet, hands and heart, it is I who does the work. I vow this day to see only abundance, think only abundance, and celebrate the miracle found within me.

from my heart . . .

Within ourselves is the cause of the disorder in our own individual world for we each live in a little world of our own creation.

—Henry Thomas Hamblin

We Are All Beggars of Some Sort

My acquaintance with the "big" city was as abrupt as the blizzard of 1996 in Washington, D.C. I was startled and depressed by the disheartening presence of poverty nestled in the midst of the city's glitz and glamour. Beggars were as commonplace as designer jeans. Needing money for food, shelter and any items deemed necessary to eke out a palatable existence, while trying to grasp the hidden meaning under all of this, many accepted panhandling as the only way to survive.

Daily, I watched people with kind expressions on their faces pass needy individuals as if they were some alien life form. Remembering one of the most powerful laws of prosperity, never miss an opportunity to give, I tried to help, but it was not long before I realized I could not help them all.

I know our thoughts create our experiences, but even some of the best truth teachers admit that social conditions do have an impact on our lives, thereby, making us all responsible. Something in this human machine we created produces more and more people who end up living on the streets. We must seriously ask "Are my hands clean?"

The Course of Miracles says the things we see in the outer represent what we collectively believe to be true in the inner. Because our thoughts have power, our own consciousness is destroying the core of our society.

If we pay close attention to our lives and our thoughts, we will see that we are all beggars of some sort.

Not unlike the homeless, hungry and displaced in our society, we are continually trying to fill a void. Even though we do not lack shelter or food in the literal sense, we often find our souls in the midst of a spiritual drought.

We are constantly begging and beseeching Spirit for more money, better health, perfect children, great relationships, the perfect weight, perfect jobs, and so on and so forth. Spirit should be as weary of our begging as we have become of the downtrodden who have made their homes on the streets of our cities.

Embracing Life's Lessons

We are created with the power of the Divine Mind. Because the essence of Spirit is love, we are given all we need to satisfy our thirst, hunger and to set right all human errors.

Since society is a reflection of our collective consciousness, survival is dependent upon our commitment to clean our mental and spiritual closets. Ridding ourselves of anger and truly devoting our lives to discovering inner peace, will collectively eliminate violence in our communities. Florence Schinn said that everyone reaches a point where they cannot see the truth about themselves. It is during these times that others, who hold in mind for you your true identity, will help you overcome these trials. Being determined to see the Christ Spirit in everyone we meet will encourage our brothers and sisters to see themselves as they truly are, a perfect idea in the mind of the Creator. Once everyone starts to embrace their perfection, our society can began to heal. Remember, it is said that there is enough good in the worst of us, and enough bad in the best of us, that it hardly behooves any of us, to judge the rest of us.

As you embrace your perfection, promise yourself that you will be too kind for anger, too strong for fear and too happy for worry. After all, life is too short to drink cheap champagne.

Meditation/Affirmative Prayer

Recognizing that I am more powerful than I will ever know, I alone am able to alter the effects of race consciousness. I will encourage my brothers and sisters by first encouraging myself.

I will positively affect societies ills by first knowing that I already have the money, success and beauty I pray for. I will also know for myself that as I change my thoughts, I change my world.

I will change the world by exuding this confidence and living a life filled with the goodness of God. Then and only then can I teach by example.

from my heart . . .

I permeate all the universe in my unmanifest form. All beings exist within me, yet I am so inconceivably vast, so beyond existence.

—Bhagavad Gita, Translator-Stephen Mitchell

The Problem

The journey to discover my true essence has taken many uncharted twists and turns. The majority of the time, I am able to refresh my soul with lectures, lessons and books that are uplifting and espouse the absolute good that is Spirit. But there are still times when my soul cries out for a gut-wrenching stanza or two of "precious Lord, take my hand." These times are more frequent than I would like to acknowledge but less frequent than when I decide the path to travel without first consulting the Divine Allness.

As I go through new challenges, I realize nothing is impossible, except in my own consciousness, and it is my limited vision that must first be overcome.

When I remember Spirit's promise to Jacob, "I will not leave you . . . until I have done what I promised," I am touched by Jacob's reaction: "this is none other than the house of God." I then recognize that challenges and appearances are the gates of heaven, and immediately, I am guided back into right thinking.

Every minute of our lives we are choosing between love and fear, heaven and hell, littleness and glory, lack and plenty. As we venture into the unexplored territory within, we will soon understand that nothing has changed. Spirit is always being Spirit. The question is do we believe this, and are we able to completely embody this principle? As we allow the ego to gather momentum and solidify the belief that we are separate from Spirit, quickly our human experience attempts to discipline our thoughts, words, and actions until we are able to do it ourselves.

I once believed we needed more time. But if Spirit is, then Spirit has no use for time. What Spirit wants is our acknowledgement, our consent, our willingness to believe that It lives in us, as us and is us.

Because the Creator is omniscient, it is instant. There is no need to want anything because we have already been given the gifts of Heaven. Therefore, times only use is that we make room for the

Embracing Life's Lessons

abundance awaiting our discovery. We eagerly accept meager substitutes and unknowingly embrace limiting beliefs which serve as fertilizer for turbulent conditions to take hold in our experience. We cannot simultaneously believe in the promises of Spirit and in the power of outer appearances.

I have experienced some of the worst conditions possible. Being unemployed and practically homeless lasted nearly a year, and at every turn people were quick to remind me that "I had worked all my life and did not have a thing to show for it." Those who did not say it to me were saying it to everybody else. Having tried everything possible to find work, I gave up. One night during meditation, I was reminded that every experience is created twice: once in the mind and again in the outer. At this point, I decided to concentrate on healing my imagined separation from the Omnipotent and not the situation that appeared because of this belief. I studied truth lessons and twice a day just sat in the silence. I did not ask Spirit for a job or a place to stay. I just asked to become more aware of the Divine Presence. Each hour I would spend a few minutes reaffirming my oneness with Spirit. Soon, I was chatting nonstop with Spirit. The nights were not as dark, the tears less frequent and the bouts of loneliness began to ease. Magically, the perfect job with perfect pay seemed to "drop out of the ethers." This manifestation filled my soul with gratitude and a quiet knowing enfolded me. With Spirit nothing is impossible.

Meditation/Affirmative Prayer

When my soul cries out "Father why have you forsaken me?" I will use this as a reminder to "let go or be dragged," and release any attachment to preconceived outcomes.

Spirit has determined my purpose and my path. I will teach my ego that God is all there, so every outcome is filled with blessings.

Today as I concentrate on the goodness of life, I remember nothing is impossible.

from my heart . . .

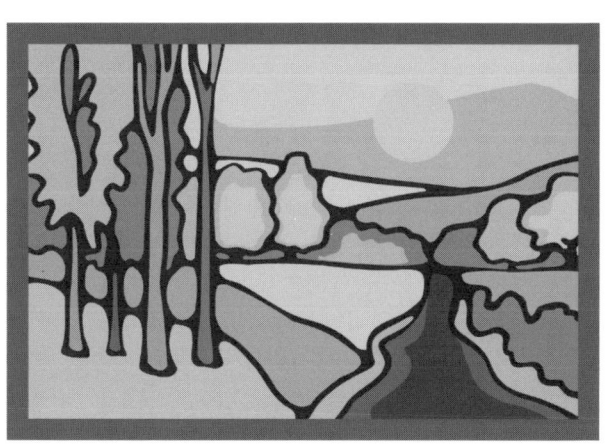

The ABCs of Prosperity

*A*ccentuate the positive and *A*ccept only the best.

*B*elieve that you can achieve your hearts desire.

*C*reate a vacuum. *C*onstantly rid your life of toxic relationships.

*D*are to dream big and don't look back.

*E*veryday, work toward your dreams.

*F*orgive and *F*orget your mistakes as well as the mistakes of others. Give more of what you need.

*H*old steadfast to your dreams in the face of adversity.

*I*mage often the result you want.

*J*udge no one. *J*udge no thing. *J*udge no situation.

Keep the end in sight. Don't focus on the process.

Learn to see only good in all things.

Meditate to keep your mind in tune to the will of Spirit.

Never concentrate on negative things or situations.

Obey divine guidance.

Pray like it all depends on God.

Quietly work on your dreams; talking about them hinders your progress.

Revise and update your plans and goals constantly.

Stay focused. Keep the main thing the main thing.

Trust in Spirit and the process of the Universe unconditionally.

Understand things are not as they appear to be and appearances are never real.

Victory is for those who are diligent.

Work like it all depends on you.

Xpect to win.

You are a magnificent creation of the universe.

Zealously live your life and and remember life is too short to drink cheap champagne.

From the Author's Heart . . .

AFTERWORD

Embracing Life's Lessons by Stephanie E. Wilson encourages one to live Life's Lessons to the fullest. Each chapter suggests how uniquely the author has embraced her lessons (challenges and opportunities) in life.

It is a biography of a purposeful life. Each chapter illustrates a spiritual awakening and is followed by a meditation/affirmation that assists in the positive resolution of the lesson.

HOW THE BOOK WILL HELP THE READER? It will help the reader to identify what has or what is happening in his or her life and the lesson or lessons that are available to assist in overcoming any challenge or opportunity victoriously. It is easy to read. You may read one or two chapters that you can identify with, and discover a solution to your challenge to dream big dreams.

HOW EASY IS IT TO FOLLOW? *Embracing Life's Lessons* is easy to read and follow because the author gives directives through her examples in each chapter. She has incorporated living Life's Lessons by embracing them with the Spirit and Love of God in each chapter. She emphasizes that as we live through our lessons in living, our goals and dreams will be fulfilled by the Creator.

Rev. Whilmetta D. Harrell
Staff Minister of Christ Universal Temple
Editor of Daily Inspiration for Better Living
Universal Foundation for Better Living

To order additional books
or for further information, contact:

Distributed by:
Baker and Taylor Books

or

Stephanie E. Wilson
P. O. BOX 87468
Chicago, IL 60680
773-241-5683

website:
www.champagneconnection.com

e-mail address:
stephanie.wilson@champagneconnection.com
or
champagne102@hotmail.com